BETH NEAL

Notes To You

A messy and magical journey of motherhood.

First published by Beth Neal 2025

Copyright © 2025 by Beth Neal

All rights reserved. No part of this publication may be reproduced, stored in a retrieval system, or transmitted to any form or by any means-electronic, photocopying, recording, or otherwise without prior written permission from the author.

This is a work of nonfiction based on personal experience. Names and identifying details may have been changed to protect privacy.

Beth Neal asserts the moral right to be identified as the author of this work.

Cover design by Beth Neal.

Some design elements used are under license from Canva.

First edition

ISBN (print): 978-1-7644283-0-9
ISBN (digital): 978-1-7644283-2-3

This book was professionally typeset on Reedsy.
Find out more at reedsy.com

Contents

Introduction	1
A Note to Mothers Before	4
A Note of Love	5
Sorry in Advance	6
Before	7
Pregnancy	11
Labour	32
Birth Preferences	42
Image Break	43
Notes to my Daughter	55
Now	98
A Note to Myself	100
A Note of Thanks	102
Connection	104

Introduction

My mother and I use to leave notes on the kitchen table for each other:
 "Happy Tuesday, see you after work!"
 "Thank you for helping me with my homework."
 "Big loves x".

These notes are irreplaceable.
I keep them just as safe as I keep my birth certificate or passport.

This is a consolidation of my thoughts and feelings about my experience of motherhood so far, mostly in note form.

A note from Mah.

For the loving parent who only has time to read just one paragraph at a time…
For the mother who doesn't enjoy pregnancy and needs a new perspective or something to look forward to…
For the mother who didn't enjoy pregnancy, but has a heart full of love for their baby…
For anyone who takes the time to read…
   Thank you.

Here are some of my perhaps un-popular opinions, I wish I knew were 'normal' during my journey.

Introduction

Raw, heart-warming and funny.
  Probably in that order.

A Note to Mothers Before

I'm sorry.

I'm sorry I didn't see you.

I thought I was visiting your baby and celebrating that new life.

I didn't know what you had given, nor could I have fathomed what you went through.

I didn't see *you*.

I should have hugged you first.
I should have bought you coffee.
I should have let you know how incredible you are.
I simply should have done more.

I didn't know then, but I do now.
I see you and I promise to pay it forward.

A Note of Love

Inspired by my mother.
Supported by my husband.
Dedicated to my child.

Sorry in Advance

Hi Grandma,
   Sorry in advance for swearing!

Before

We got married in May.

Our next step was a family.

The following week I had my Intrauterine Device (contraceptive IUD) removed.

"It is possible for you to fall pregnant before your next cycle…" the nurse told me.

Wouldn't that be lucky?

8 weeks later.

I'm interstate with my husband and our 2 just married friends.

We are all about to go scuba diving.

Completing the health questionnaire:

"Are you pregnant?" no [×] … surely not, right?

Maybe I should take a test when we get home…

At home a few nights later, I realise I'm late. Only 1 day…

I go to bed and have a dream; I hear voices telling me "Pregnant".

Faint at first but then louder and louder. I wake up in the night thinking about it.

Weird.

I need to get a pregnancy test tomorrow.

I have been feeling snotty and ill all day.

It's about 5pm.

How can I leave the house on my own, without my husband wanting to come with me?

Could I just tell him I'm late?

No.

I want to surprise him if it's positive.

I do feel sick.

I'll say I'm getting some lozenges.

Mission accomplished.

I sneak upstairs and pee on the stick… oh my God.

"Pregnant."

I stare at the test for about 5 minutes.

Laughing.

Crying.

So much joy.

I don't believe it.

Now to tell my husband.

I had thought about this moment for years.

I always wanted to hide a note inside of a Kinder Surprise chocolate egg, so when he opened it, he would read "You're going to be a Dad!"

Why didn't I buy chocolate eggs when I bought the test?

I'll just buy some tomorrow and tell him then.

Before

No, I can't wait that long.

I'll run downstairs with the test and show him now!

But I really want to surprise him with the note in the chocolate egg…

There is *no* chance I can make up something to get out of the house to go to the shops, again.

"We need eggs for dinner!" I hear from downstairs.

No way.

What a coincidence.

Ok, I bought eggs.

Real eggs for dinner and Kinder Surprise eggs for my announcement.

I also got some baby socks - I'll roll up a baby sock with the note around it.

I go upstairs with my things to practice dissembling the chocolate eggs.

I bought a few for good measure.

It was surprisingly easy.

I only needed 1.

My husband puts on a movie while we eat dinner.

There's a husband and a wife, and the wife announces she is pregnant.

I try to act nonchalant.

How weird.

After dinner I clean up and get the pre-assembled chocolate egg.

"Do you want some chocolate?" I call out.

"Yes please!"

Good.
I can't wait to see his reaction.

I give my husband the chocolate and wait.
He talks to me while eating.
Oh my God! Hurry up!
He's talking about some video game he is playing and how the characters blah blah blah…
Shut up and eat!
When he finally opens it, the note falls to the floor.
He doesn't notice!
But then; "A baby sock. Weird!" He holds it up and shows me.
I nervously laugh, "huh….so weird."
…
…
"Are you fucking pregnant!?"
I can't speak. I nod and laugh. Nervous and excited.
"Really?"
I keep nodding and pull out the positive test.
"That's beautiful! I'm so proud of us!"
He holds me close as he keeps taking it in.
He's going to be a great dad!

Pregnancy

I was somewhere between 3 and 4 weeks when I found out I was pregnant.
Though it seems to be common practice, we did not wait until week 12, or even our first ultrasound, to tell the ones we love. We told people early to create a support system. If we were to go to our ultrasound and find out I had a miscarriage, we would be grieving in silence, pretending nothing happened. Waiting until week 12 and not telling anyone until then does not prevent anything bad from happening. So we decide to tell each of our mothers first. Both know before week 5. We tell our close friends and family as soon as we can. They all know by week 7.

When I was pregnant I felt alienated.
    I so wish that I knew it was OK to simultaneously feel grateful but not enjoy the ride.

Man this nausea sucks…

Why does all food smell disgusting?
Don't even talk to me about dinner…
gag

I try to hide my pregnancy and symptoms at work.

Nearly impossible.

Then lunchtime comes and I can smell people's food wafting from microwaves.

Definitely impossible.

The nausea hits like a brick wall! I run to the bathroom and spend my entire lunch break vomiting.

To get to the bathroom from my desk I need to walk through my bay, walk down the hall, past another 2 bays, through the kitchen, through a sliding door, past elevators, then I finally reach the bathroom.

This would be far easier to manage at home…

After a day or two, people either think I have gastro or they have already pieced together that I'm pregnant.

"Can I work from home full time for a few weeks while I try to hide my pregnancy symptoms?" I request from work.

"No, you need to be in the office."

Excuse me? Why are the higher ups arguing this?

"If I work from home I can hide my symptoms, which I'd like to do. I don't want the office knowing early. Plus, I won't need to worry about making it to the bathroom when I'm sick." I defend, not that I think I should need to.

"When your co-workers were pregnant they didn't get to work from home."

Irrelevant but sure, that was years ago.

"All that does is make me feel sorry for them for not being adequately supported."

Pregnancy

"You can do half days in the office."

"Sure."

It doesn't help.

Despite my best efforts, work finds out about my pregnancy early.

My manager and colleagues are ecstatic when they find out. "You only just got married!"

"Ha, I know."

We didn't waste any time.

They check in with me regularly but I'm pretty moody.

I have been sick all day. I don't think I can make it to our first ultrasound. Should I reschedule? No. Surely nauseous women have appointments all the time, right?

We hear our baby's heart beat for the first time. It's magic! I nervous laugh with relief.

Suddenly, the nausea vanishes. My husband has such a big smile on his face, he looks at me and holds my hand tight.

I'm glad I didn't reschedule.

My husband and I don't want to find out the baby's gender until birth.

We share bank accounts, we give each other wish lists for birthdays and Christmas, we tell each other everything. Nothing is a true 'surprise'.

But this will be.

My boobs hurt. They're getting bigger.

I've always had a smaller chest. Throughout the rest of my pregnancy and getting my baby bump, I joke that I actually have

3 baby bumps.

We just received a meal kit box. Our groceries are organised for a whole week. The only thing is, I feel repulsed by all of it.
All I feel like today is a cheeseburger.

The next day the thought of a cheeseburger is enough to make me feel sick.
Nuggets seem fine... but specifically KFC nuggets.
The next day it has to be McDonald's nuggets.

I don't really have any cravings over the 9 months of pregnancy. It's more of a 'I feel like this food today because it won't make me vomit' feeling.

Me, a mother? But *I* don't know everything. *My* mum knows everything. If I don't know how to do something, I ask my mum. She *always* knows. How am I supposed to be that for my baby? I cant even boil an egg.
Truly. I can't.
I still ask my mum to boil eggs for me.
I have tried and tried.
I've tried every method you can name.
I've read how, watched YouTube tutorials and Tiktoks, even tried an air fryer!
I can't.
My mum got me an egg boiling machine while I was pregnant. Supposedly makes perfect boiled eggs every time.
I try it straight away but the smell of eggs makes me vomit.
I put the machine away. Maybe one day I'll try again.

Pregnancy

I'm so hungry! But the thought of eating is unappealing and actually eating makes me sick. But I'm so hungry my stomach hurts. And it feels like the hunger is making the nausea worse.

I try plain foods; plain pasta, rice cakes…

But they come back up.

The constant balance of nausea and hunger persist like a battle of survival.

In the back of my mind I worry whether the baby is getting what it needs, even when I can't keep food down.

Ugh.

I'm 13 weeks when we have the second ultrasound. Everything is looking great and the baby is healthy. The baby was like a little jumping bean! It wouldn't stay still - which was crazy because I hadn't felt any kicks yet. How was all this movement happening and I had no idea? The baby stops moving for long enough to get a photo, then off it goes again. If this is any indicator for the future, I will certainly have my hands full.

We were fortunate enough to get into an amazing pregnancy program. We were assigned a midwife to be our point of contact and we have regular check ups and information classes. And when the baby comes, we will have home visits to check on us all. My husband and I feel incredibly supported and as informed as we can be for what lies ahead. Every time we see our midwife I have a thousand silly questions about my symptoms: "Is this normal?", "Is that normal?", "I don't like this, is there something wrong with me?" Not once does she make me feel silly; she always meets me with the compassion and validation I so need. I am provided with appropriate physical and mental health support.

Even with all the support tools under my belt, I still struggle.
 Even so, I'm so grateful for all the support around me. Unfortunately, our midwife was unwell during the birth of our baby, but the midwives that took care of us instead were equally incredible.

My anxiety is already high on a good day. Now, I'm having panic attacks at least every second day. My head is full of worry like a never ending haze.
 I cry every day.
 Whether I can hide it or not is a different story - while driving, while grocery shopping, during my lunch breaks, in the work bathroom, in bed when my husband thinks I have gone to sleep early, at events, any time and anywhere. I'm unsure if I ever really stopped.
 Should I increase my meds? I hope not.
 If I am this anxious now, I can't imagine how I'll be when the baby comes.
 Anxiety is the wrong word. I feel paranoid.

I hate being pregnant. Have I said that already? I might mention it a few more times, just in case. I always thought I would love it.
 Why? I don't know. Maybe because society tells us that's how it should be.
Maybe I thought I'd "glow". Maybe I thought I'd look cute. Maybe I thought I'd love feeling the little kicks. Maybe because I hadn't really heard anyone complain about it before?
 I don't love it.

Pregnancy

I hate it!

I do appreciate my pregnancy, absolutely. It is not lost on me how amazing my body is. How lucky we are…

But I don't enjoy the ride. During my pregnancy, both my baby and I have been A-OK physically. No complications. For this I am so very grateful and I try to remind myself how fortunate we are.

I worry about my husband and our marriage. People say it's common for parents to separate after children. I grew up with separated parents and my parents did too. How will I prioritise my marriage and a baby if I can't even keep it together right now?

I don't like my body. It's changing too much.
   But it should change. It needs to change.
   I see myself and think 'I can't look in the mirror today.'
   I don't look in the mirror most days.

Before being pregnant I had a complicated relationship with my body image.
   Distorted image of myself, poor relationship with food… That's normal, right?
   Despite all the work I have done to love myself, all the body changes during pregnancy
   were extremely confronting.
   I have never heard anyone talk about these struggles resurfacing while pregnant.
   It's tough.
   But of course I look after myself. I'm responsible for more than just me now.

It's just another battle in my head that I try to fight.

In 2017 I had an unexplained blood clot in my eye, which caused a permanent loss of partial vision. This also played into my anxiety during pregnancy.

At the time, I lost count of the amount of blood tests I had done to try and find an answer. I had MRIs done. I saw an ophthalmologist, haematologist and cardiologist. Yet, no conclusive answers were given. The blood clot caused irreversible damage to the tissue in my eye and all I was told by medical professionals was "We don't know why."

Somewhere along the way, one of the specialists told me that if I ever had children, I would likely have a recurrence of the blood clot.

Great. What did that mean?

Will I lose more of my sight?

Will I lose the baby?

I almost convince myself something bad will happen so I can detach.

So it will hurt less if something goes wrong.

Luckily, I am told I have a low-risk pregnancy, but that doesn't stop the doubt from creeping in.

I woke up because I stretched too hard.

These foot cramps are insane.

I go to have my glucose tolerance test, to test for gestational diabetes. I have to fast overnight and when I arrive I scull a sugary drink which tastes like syrup. I feel instantly nauseated.

I have to wait around for a few hours so they can regularly test my blood sugar.

Pregnancy

While I'm waiting I feel the baby go wild. It feels like a little tornado, like anyone looking in my direction would be able to see my belly moving.

The test results are favourable and the baby has its first sugar high.

About halfway through my pregnancy I can eat without being sick, and I have a huge appetite.

When I feel hungry I have approximately 5 minutes to eat something before I feel ravenous. I almost always have a snack in hand or a meal near by.

For lunch one day I make myself some noodles.

"Whoa you had two packets of noodles! You must be eating for two!"

I would have had 2 packets of noodles prior to being pregnant.

I smile and nervously laugh.

"Yeah."

I don't mention that I have already had a banana, yoghurt, strawberries, muesli bar, grapes, biscuits and a sandwich…

Not to mention I have leftover dinner to heat up later…

Yeah, 2 packets of noodles is crazy…

Why do people think they can comment on my body?

Why do people think they can touch my body?

"You don't mind if I touch the baby do you?" They proceed to touch me.

"Actually yes, I do mind. You're touching me. Not the baby."

They look offended.

Seriously…?

I could roll my eyes into next week.

I already had 2 bulging discs. Pregnancy isn't letting me forget that.

I have sciatica. My back hurts and my legs go between numb and stinging.

My lower belly hurts. Is that 'round ligament pain'?

I am *so* short of breath. Is it my asthma? Is it the baby taking up space?

I can't walk and talk without sounding like I'm running a marathon.

I am exhausted.

Why is it so hard to walk to the toilet?

I struggle to wipe myself. How much space is this baby taking up?

How much more helpless can I feel?

I have no energy.

I feel heavy.

A year ago I had laser hair removal but the hair has grown back.

(Spoiler, after the baby is born, the hair stops growing again. Hormones are wild).

My ribs hurt.

I'm having heart palpitations, daily.

I can't take a full breath.

I have indigestion.

I'm hungry but have no room to eat - at least I'm not throwing up anymore.

My nose is always blocked and runny.

I'm mouth breathing.

My mouth is dry.

My breath smells.

I have thrush.

Pregnancy

I smell - I can smell myself.
I change my underwear about 3 times a day.
Am I growing a skin tag?
I have diarrhoea.
I'm hot all the time and can't stop sweating.
I wake up every night in pools of my own sweat.
My feet are cramping.
Huh? Is that another skin tag?

Will my husband still find me attractive after the baby? How will my body look then? I don't love myself now. How will I love myself when baby is born?

People feel entitled to touch my belly when they see me and comment on my body.

People comment on what I eat and how much I eat.

Leave me alone!

I'm not looking after myself very well. I know I need to change that. But the baby is OK. Maybe looking after myself means rest? Maybe I *am* looking after myself? Maybe I'm not doing enough?

I'm so anxious I can't sleep. I'm so exhausted I can't stay awake.

If I do sleep, I wake up more exhausted than when I went to sleep.

These symptoms are not one at a time. They're all present every day.

I need to ask for help, a lot.

Almost everything is a pregnancy symptom, I'm barely surprised anymore. I feel like I could google: "Is it normal for a

whale to fall out of my ass while pregnant?" and the search result would say "Yes. 9/10 women experience this!"
Duh.

I'm baffled when I hear that some women have no symptoms.
What do you mean? Where do they go?
Here. They're all on *my* bingo card.

You know what else is crazy?
When we are unwell with, lets say, a cold or gastro, we take some time off work to rest and recover. That's 1, *maybe* 2 of the listed symptoms above.
But slap on 153 other symptoms and the label of 'pregnant', then taking time to look after yourself becomes unimportant. It's society's expectation that we work through it at full capacity, and love it.
Women are incredible. We are all *Wonder Women.*

Like I said earlier, I have plenty of support, but I'm not used to asking for help. My anxiety is the worst thing. I don't know if I can do this again. We always wanted 2 children but one may be enough.
I need to tell my husband how I feel, but I'm scared… and ashamed.
I hope I don't let him down.

"Your bump looks bigger now than it did this morning!"
"Thanks. It's all the food I have eaten."
Ha, bloated or baby bump? Up until about 20 weeks, the answer is bloated.

Pregnancy

At our third and final ultrasound at 22 weeks the baby is head down and we struggle to get a photo of its head. Instead, we get a photo of the baby's feet. We are told that the baby is in the 33rd percentile, but I'm reassured this is not a bad thing and they're growing perfectly fine.

From now until birth we won't see our baby, but we do hear its heart beat through a doppler at our midwife appointments. Our midwife also feels around for baby's position and each visit confirms that the baby is still head down.

I feel the baby get hiccups all the time.

At first, I thought it was muscle spasms or something.

Why am I doing that?

Then it clicked that it was hiccups.

I can feel them through my entire pelvic floor, including my butt.

Why does no-one talk about this either?

Probably because it's weird to tell people: "You'll feel baby hiccups in your butt hole."

"The baby is kicking!"

"Isn't it amazing how much love we have for babies before we even meet them?"

Huh.

I don't think I love the baby... not yet.

At the moment I don't know if I do love it.

Actually, I do know - I don't. To say "I *think* I don't" just feels more forgiving.

I don't like being pregnant. I don't like all the discomfort, being reliant on help, feeling alien to myself, having panic attacks all the time. I'm disconnecting myself from the experience.

Inevitably, I am also disconnecting from the baby.

Will I love my baby when its born? What if I don't? I don't deserve this miracle. So many families struggle, and we didn't. I should be grateful. Stop being negative. I'm an awful mother. I'm letting my husband down. I'm letting my baby down.

These strings of thought haunt me for the rest of my pregnancy.

Would finding out the gender help? Would I feel more connected knowing I can say "he" or "she", "son" or "daughter"?

To know its name?

To have its clothes ready?

To set up the nursery?

I don't know. Maybe it would help. Maybe it wouldn't.

I find the courage to voice all of my paranoia to my husband.

I cry so much while getting out the words, I can barely get out one sentence at a time.

The guilt and shame is overwhelming.

He sits and listens.

He holds my hand, then he holds me.

Not one single time does he place judgement, blame or even try to twist my perspective.

He listens. He validates me and tells me I am enough.

He reminds me of what an amazing thing I am doing and how much he appreciates me.

Every day he asks, "What do you need from me today?"

Every day he tells me how much he loves me.

Every day he tells me I'm beautiful.

Pregnancy

I almost believe him.
How did I get so lucky?

There have been a few times where I have felt reduced fetal movement.

We go to hospital and they monitor baby's movement and heart rate. The baby is totally fine, just having a lazy day I guess. The whole time all I can think to myself is "Please be OK, please be OK".

So I know I care for the baby, but *'love'* still seems foreign.

Usually, my self-care is exercise. I love the gym, yoga, pilates and outdoor walks. My husband and I met at Muay Thai. But while pregnant I have no energy for any of that.

If I can't look after myself while pregnant, how could I ever have a second baby?

How could I look after this baby while going through this again?

I don't know if I can.

All I can manage is about ten minutes of static stretching each day.

With that comes meditation and breathing.

I do my best but some days even that feels too much to manage.

I was gifted a pregnancy journal. It will remain empty.

I can't bring myself to write in it and pretend to enjoy this.

Instead, maybe one day I'll put all my thoughts on paper and someone out there will read and relate…

But not in that journal.

Notes To You

By a similar vein, I struggle with the idea of getting pregnancy photos done. I don't recognise myself and I don't feel beautiful. I don't want to immortalise these feelings.

At 8 months, a close family member takes some photos for us. Surprisingly, for the first time in my whole pregnancy, I feel beautiful. We have 1 of the photos printed and hanging on our wall. I'm very grateful for the photos.

Everyone I speak to seems to have loved being pregnant. They also say how hard parenting is. If I already think pregnancy is hard, how will I cope when the baby is here?

"How are you feeling?" People ask me.
"I'm OK. Tired, sore…" I don't say I hate it.
They laugh.
"Just wait! If you think you're tired now, just wait until the baby is here."
Are you trying to help me, or scare me?

"Sleep now while you can."
Thanks, I'll put all of my overtime sleep into the bank and withdraw it when I need some extra hours at 3am.

"Sleep when the baby sleeps."
OK. And I guess I'll shower when the baby showers, do groceries when the baby does groceries and cook dinner when the baby cooks dinner?

"You'll forget all about it and you'll do it all again!"
Huh. Will I?
Thanks for telling me how I'll feel…

Pregnancy

Maybe I will. But that's not for anyone else to say.

Don't complain. Keep it to yourself. Or maybe, write it out in a book one day.

Has anyone ever disliked pregnancy?
Am I the only one?
What's wrong with me?

Before my husband and I start our parental leave, both of our workplaces generously gift us some vouchers and baby accessories. My work organises a small lunch to celebrate and they participate in an 'advice card' activity.
The most common piece of advice: Remember you love each other.

We have a baby shower in the summer. It's in our complex.
Some children see me setting up some decorations.
"Can we watch your gender reveal?"
"I'm sorry, I'm not doing one."
"Oh. Do you even live here?"
I laugh to myself. Sorry to disappoint you.
We have our close friends and family come to celebrate our baby. We are showered with so much love and generosity. This baby is already surrounded by the best people.
Our guests decorate blocks for the baby (an idea I found on the internet). They take their guesses on boy or girl by placing a pink or blue fingerprint as a leaf on a tree.
We have advice cards for guests to write on - they can also guess the date of birth and give name suggestions.
Most people guess boy.

No-one guesses any of the names we like.
And no-one guesses the arrival date.

My 2 favourite pieces of advice:
Don't put the baby down. Hold them close for as long as you can.
Don't try to make a happy baby happier.

My husband and I can agree on a boy name. 2 or 3 actually, but we have always had one in particular ready to go.
"What do you think of this name for a girl?" I ask my husband.
"Nah."
A few weeks go by and my husband says, "What do you think of this name for a girl?"
My eye twitches. It's the same name I suggested and he declined.
"Yes. Great name."

We are generously gifted a box of newborn nappies. There's 96.
"Cool! We have nappies for the first ninety-six days." My husband says.
"Do you think babies use just one nappy a day?"
We stock up on more.
Similarly, we have several outfits in newborn size. My husband says we don't need more clothes, we have enough for 1 outfit a day.
This is where I realised he doesn't know how messy babies can be.

I guess something funny during pregnancy is 'pregnancy brain'.
I can attribute the silly things I do to it. Play ignorant, if you

will.

I make a meeting at work and title it "15 minute catch up". The meeting goes for 30 minutes. This is deliberate because the time slots default to 30 minutes, and I'm too lazy to take the 8 seconds to input the 15 minute difference. Besides, the extra time can be overtime in case of IT issues or questions.

"You know you wrote 15 minutes but it goes for 30!?"

Yes.

"Ha, oh this pregnancy brain is silly!" I can't be bothered explaining.

I hear all about it for the rest of the day.

Then it really kicks in;

I put groceries away and put cashews in the fridge.

Weird, but not that bad.

I make myself a coffee, the bin drawer is open as I pour milk… I accidentally pour some milk into the bin… I get a cloth to clean it up… but there's no mess. What is this, why can't I think straight? I finally put milk in my coffee. Put my coffee in the fridge and take my milk to the couch with me.

Uh… what have I done? Oops.

I love the smell of my husband. His face in particular. I go up to him randomly, shove my nose into his cheek and inhale. Mmmm.

Um, is this normal? Is this what I'll be like with the baby and sniffing it's head?

In early pregnancy before I had a belly, when I was out of the house I'd think to myself "No one knows I'm pregnant." It was a funny little secret I had.

In late pregnancy when my husband and I are out, I jokingly ask him:

"Do you think anyone can tell I'm pregnant?"

"You can't see your own toes or bend down to put shoes on."

"So… is that a yes?"

We laugh.

At some point I decided it would be a good idea to quiz my husband on my medical history. At random points through the day I interrupt:

"What medication do I take?"

"Anxiety tablets."

"What am I allergic to?"

"Penicillin."

"What happens if I take penicillin?"

"You get a blistery rash."

It takes a few repetitions to remember the answers, but he remembers none the less.

How will I know if the baby is too cold? How will I know if the baby is too hot? How will I know if the baby stops breathing?

Are there baby monitors to detect these things?

Yes.

Which monitor is the best?

Which device is the best?

What if it runs out of battery?

Should I have 2 just in case?

For the unknown-th time, I am losing sleep over this.

Pregnancy

At least I finish work soon.

I can focus on myself and relax before the baby comes.

37 weeks + 4 days pregnant, I'm positive for covid.

Great.

Covid aggravated my breathlessness; I struggled to even roll over in bed. Was it asthma, the baby taking up lung capacity, covid or all 3? It felt like someone was sitting on my chest. One moment I would be dripping sweat and the next I would be shivering cold. Flipping my blanket on and off every minute. I hadn't felt the baby move much. Was it because *I* wasn't moving much? Was the baby sick too?

We go to hospital just to make sure.

They monitor the baby and do some blood tests.

"Your baby is totally fine."

The doctor tells me that my baby will get all the antibodies that my body is producing.

That's good.

"You're just going to have a shit few days."

Oh, shitter than I already feel? Great.

I already had no energy and somehow now I had even less. I stay in bed and sleep for the next few days. Not that I would have been doing much else anyway.

Labour

39 weeks + 5 days

It's a Tuesday.

We are having dinner at our friends' house. Home made curry. Delicious! I sit down to eat.

pop

What was that? My legs are wet. Lucky I'm sitting down. I'll eat first then check.

This curry is delicious.

I go to the bathroom. I'm wearing pink bike shorts. Both inner legs are wet and discoloured down to my knees. Did anyone see or notice my shorts when I got up? How embarrassing.

Did my water break? Maybe I should call my midwife.

"It sounds like your waters could have broken."

I monitor for symptoms of labour until we go to see our midwife the next morning.

Labour

"I'm going into work until our appointment then I will start my leave." My husband tells me he's finishing a few things at work and then leaving.

"Your waters didn't break."
 What?
 The midwife and doctors did 3 tests to check if the liquid leak was amniotic fluid.
 It wasn't.
 What was it then? I didn't wee myself.

40 weeks + 2 days
It's been almost a week.
 "If the baby isn't here by Monday then I'll go back to work".
 I can hear the reluctance in my husband's voice.
 I mean, I'll do what I can but no promises.

40 weeks + 3 days
3am: I need to poop.

4am: Why does my stomach still ache?

5am: Is this labour? I download an app to monitor the pains and see if they are contractions.

7am: I wake my husband, "I think I'm in labour."
 "Really?"
 "Yeah. I found this app, look."
 My husband sighs with relief, "I don't have to go back to work tomorrow!"

So far contractions have been pretty mild. Like I need to go to the toilet or have a light cramp. They are just my body saying 'hello' at this point.

Even though it's early labour, I make myself focus and breathe through the contractions, no matter how small. Hopefully this helps me fall into a good habit for active labour.

I message my mum:
"I'm in labour!"

Message from mum:
"Oh my God! Exciting!"

I go about my day as normal.
I have breakfast. I shower. I potter around. I watch some TV. I shower again…
Where is this baby?

Message from mum:
"How are things?"
"Still at home. No baby yet."

12pm: I try to nap.

12:30pm: I'm woken up by stronger contractions. I can't go back to sleep.

2pm: The contractions are strong and have fallen into a regular pattern.
About 2-3 contractions every ten minutes.

Labour

The contraction pain in my uterus is manageable. It's uncomfortable rather than painful.

But it's wrapping around to my back and down my legs.

I live with chronic pain, my pain tolerance is quite high. But this back and leg pain is something else. If I have a contraction while standing I need to brace myself. I change labour positions often. Even supported positions on hands and knees, or leaning over the sofa, the pressure in my back and legs is too much and I can't support myself.

From here, I spend most of the day in and out of the shower. My husband sits with me, patiently waiting for his next order.

Warm water helps.

Until it doesn't.

Message from mum:

"At the hospital yet?"

"Not yet."

8:30pm: The pain continues to increase. Timing of contractions remains regular.

Message from mum:

"How's it all going?"

"About the same."

9:45pm: We call our midwife and tell her we are coming into the hospital.

Surely the baby is close.

Message to Mum:

"Driving to the hospital now."

On the drive to the hospital I want juice, and my husband needs something to help keep his energy up for the night ahead.

He stops at the shopping centre to get juice and an energy drink from Coles.

He will tell you that Coles was closed and he had to run around the corner to Kmart instead.

There was no juice.

Meanwhile, I'm labouring in the car, regretting waiting. Contractions were already uncomfortable, now even more so as I'm squashed in the front seat with a belt around me.

All of the twists, turns and bumps of the drive are hell.

We go over some speed bumps and I'm sure the baby has fallen out.

But that would have been too easy.

Of course we get all of the red lights.

It's nearly 10pm, why are there so many cars on the road?

10:20pm: We arrive and I don't think I can walk.

Of course I have to.

Somehow I walk through the hospital and up to the birthing suite. Our room is set up with a hot bath waiting.

I need to vomit…

False alarm.

I want to rest. I try a few positions. Everything is uncomfortable.

Labour

The urge to vomit rises again but isn't enough to come.

10:30pm: I sit in the bath. Sweet relief.
I breathe and hum through the contractions, like a meditation. It worked for a time. But the hum soon turned into grunts.

My husband sits by my side the whole time, holding my hand when I need, getting me towels and water. Every contraction he tells me how strong I am and how proud he is. I couldn't have gone through this without him. His support is unwavering.

Somewhere between 10:30pm and 1am: I ask for gas and air.
How have I gone this long without relief?
"Remember to take breaks from the gas."
Ha, *make me.*
I don't take breaks.
I vomit in the bath.

40 weeks + 4 days
1:30am: My midwife fills the bath back up and I sit in the shower while I wait. Still inhaling as much gas and air as I can.

2am: Before getting back into the bath I ask my midwife to check how dilated I am. It's been nearly 24 hours total and over 12 hours of active labour. The baby *has* to be close.
"You're 5cm…"
"Fuck off is that all!? … Sorry."
…
For the first time during labour I cry.
"I want an epidural."
I vomit again.

2:30am: "The other room is ready, it's down the hall. Would you like a wheelchair?"

"No, I'll walk."

Why the fuck did I say that? The pain in my back and legs is unbearable. That's *why* I want to be numb.

I can't walk. I'm so annoyed at myself. Why am I so stubborn? More contractions hit and I can't speak to tell anyone that I changed my mind.

It takes about 3 contractions and 10 minutes for me to walk down a short corridor.

I vomit at the front desk of the new area.

That's 3.

2:45am: "The anaesthetist is in theatre…"

Fuck. Off.

"We have called the on-call anaesthetist, we are waiting for him to come in"

Please hurry.

3:10am: The anaesthetist comes in and explains how the epidural works along with the risks.

I don't care. Do it. Hurry up and make me numb. Go!

"Before we get started, are you allergic to anything?"

A contraction hits and all I can do is grunt and groan. I can't even think of the answer, I don't know.

"Penicillin." I can hear him answering the anaesthetist's questions for me, "She gets a blistery rash. She takes medication for anxiety."

Thank goodness I quizzed him!

I love you, I love you, I love you…

I'm not sure if I'm thinking that about my husband or the

anaesthetist.

3:30am: I'm an atheist but the moment the epidural kicked in, I could have become a believer. This sweet pain free relief was a kiss from God.

Message to mum:
"Bath, vomit, shower, vomit, 5cm, vomit, epidural. No baby yet."

I got a little bit of sleep in between nurses and doctors coming in to check on me.
The epidural became uneven. I could feel (mild) contractions in my back on the right side.
I lay on my side to try even it out again. Now it's uneven on the left.
I groan. I just try to get as much rest as I can before the baby is here.

7am: 8cm and manual breaking of my waters.

8am: Hormone drip to quicken contractions.

Message from Mum:
"No baby yet!?"
"Nope. Not yet."
"This is the longest labour ever!"
"You're telling me."

10am: 10cm and I start pushing.

12pm: "We don't recommend you keep pushing past 2 hours. We will get the doctor to help with an instrumental birth."

About 20 minutes go by, by the time the doctor comes in and explains using forceps and episiotomy.

About another 10 minutes pass for her to get the equipment.

Another 5 or 10 to set up and start.

12:45pm: Holy shit the doctor is playing tug-of-war with my vagina.

The pressure is unreal.

My husband would tell you that the doctor was indeed playing tug-of-war, leaning her whole weight backwards while holding onto the forceps.

I still need to push as the doctor pulls.

But I panic. I wasn't ready for this.

On my second last push, I throw up again.

That's 4.

The tensing of my body *almost* shoots out my baby.

I nearly laugh.

12:58pm: "It's a girl!" My husband tells me while crying. He's kissing me on the forehead and staring at our daughter. "You did it! I'm so proud of you!"

Our umbilical cord was wrapped around her neck twice. The midwives and doctor quickly untangled her and my husband cut our umbilical cord. They put her on my chest and she cries. She's OK. My husband and I sob. I hear him say "She's perfect!"

Message to Mum:

Labour

"We have our baby!"

Birth Preferences

Labor as long as possible at home [check]
Water birth with minimal intervention [ha]
Epidural as my last preference [double ha]
My husband to announce gender [check]

I tried to stay away from the phrase 'birth plan'. Baby would come how baby wanted to come. And she sure did.
These were my preferences and although I knew there were other options, I had to be reminded of this during labour.

I'm very grateful how things played out.

Image Break

A drawing of our little family, by your cousin

Notes To You

baby shower guesses

Image Break

'Pac-Man' block

Notes To You

Baby block

Image Break

'Avengers' block

Waiting for you

Image Break

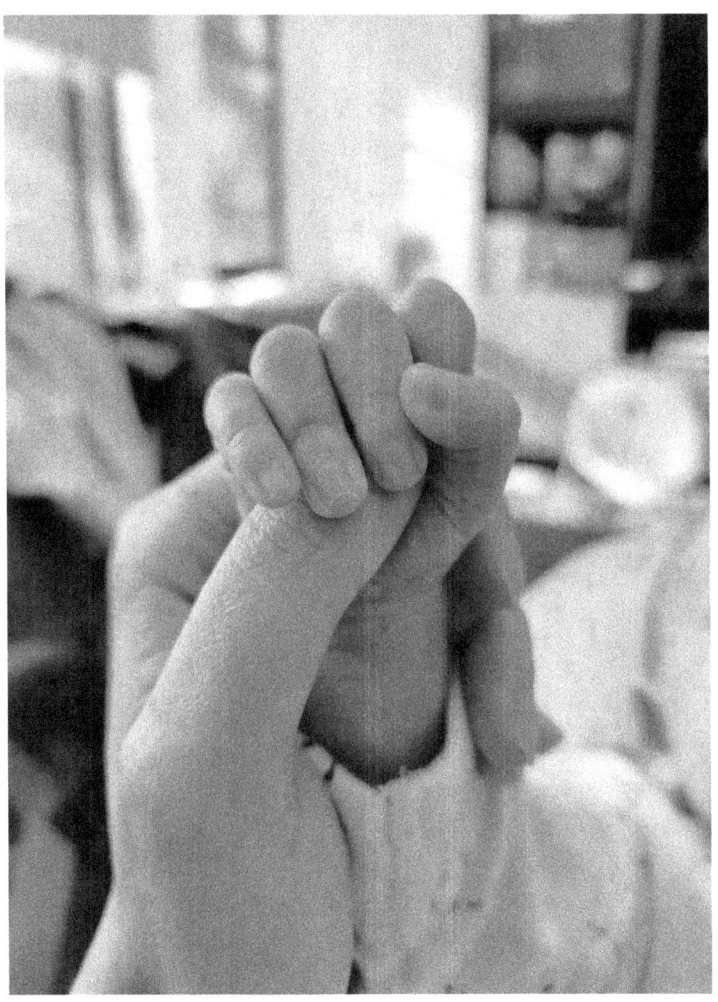

The best feeling

Notes To You

5 generations - 2025

Image Break

Bubble magic

Notes To You

Notes from Mahs

Image Break

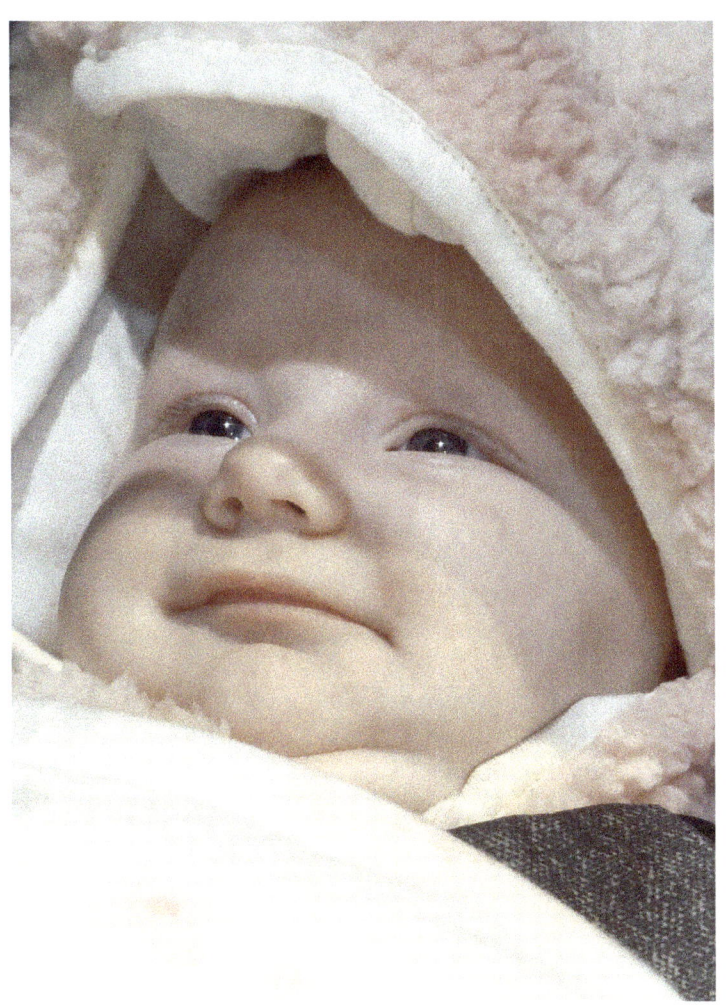

'The Blob'

Notes To You

Living the Dream

Notes to my Daughter

If love at first sight exists, then this is it.
Not only did I fall in love with you, but I fell in love again with your dad.
The way he looks at you and holds you. How he already protects and loves us is unmatched.

The moment you were born, I felt like myself again. Everything I hated in pregnancy had gone.
I love every moment of being your mum. This isn't 'hard' like I had been warned. It was an adjustment, sure. But pregnancy was hard.
This, being your Mum, is magic!

You are tiny and beautiful.
You have skin to skin with me and then with your dad.
The world became brighter and time stood still.
You are too small for your 0000 clothes.
There's a mark across your right eye from the forceps.

Your head smells like baby. You don't have much hair. Your skin is soft.

You're swaddled tight but your tiny hands escape. You love having them up by your face.

You're here. This is surreal.

You are here. I am in disbelief and awe for a long time. What a phenomenal thing my body did, to grow you and birth you. For the first time, probably in my life, I feel incredible pride in myself.

I can't wait for our friends and family to meet you.

"Look what I made!" I tell everyone.

We have a few visitors in hospital.

Some people cry.

Everyone finds out you're a girl.

Some people are surprised.

Everyone loves you.

Some say you look like your dad. Some say you look like me. I think you look like you.

You are about 12 hours old and a visitor says, "I know what's worse than child birth…"

Oh *please* enlighten me. I was just thinking to myself, 'I wish a man would come in here and completely insult everything I just experienced.'

I should have said something. Instead I look away and ignore the conversation. If my legs weren't half numb and I didn't have a catheter in, I would have taken you and walked out.

Notes to my Daughter

After our first night in hospital I woke up to your dad leaning over you, watching you sleep in your hospital bassinet. My heart skipped a beat.

In the morning a nurse comes in to check on you. I have to go to the bathroom to wee. When I walk back from the bathroom I hear farting.
Ha.
Oh. Shit… that's *me*.
I can't hold it in. My pelvic floor feels non-existent.
"I'm so sorry! I can't…"
I just laugh.
The nurse laughs too but she says it's fine.

The days go quickly.
We wake up, I look at you, I blink, and it's bed time again.
What?
Days go by in the blink of an eye.
I'm happy to spend all day looking at you.
You're gorgeous!

I find myself looking at photos of you as you sleep on me. Looking between the real you and photos of you. No matter how many times I look back and forth I still can't believe it.

Your wake windows are funny. You still don't do much. I don't know what to do with you, so we just look at each other. I don't know what you see, or how far you can see. Sometimes you smile and I'm sure it's coincidental, but I don't care. We look at each other until you fall asleep again.

When I was born, a photo was taken of 5 generations: me, my mum, my grandma, my great grandmother, and great-great grandmother.
 It was in the newspaper.
 Will you know what that is?
 You are lucky enough to also have 5 generations.
 In a few weeks, we will recreate the photo.

On our first night home, you cried in your bassinet.
 I picked you up. I held you. All night.
 I looked at you. All night.
 My eyes never left you. All night.
 I did not sleep. I was in awe. Look what I made. Look at you. Holy crap.
 What a blessing you are. Every piece of my paranoia was gone.
 You were in my arms and I couldn't be happier to stay awake all night with you.
 What a privilege it was to be the one to soothe you when you needed it.
 How is it that this unfamiliar road feels most like home?

People warned me that mothers lose their sense of identity, but I already feel more like myself than I ever have. Being the one to hold you, soothe you, clean you, raise you, is the biggest blessing. This is the most fulfilled I have ever felt.
 I think about myself and my life before you. Yes, I loved my life with your dad. But I realise now that something was missing. Not anymore.

When I birthed you, I felt re-born.

Notes to my Daughter

Raising you has been so healing. I feel that in raising you I am also raising my inner-child.

When I treat you with kindness, I treat myself with kindness.

When you need comfort, I also get comfort.

Creating a calm and safe environment for you, also creates one for me.

I don't want you to inherit the bad parts of me. The only way I can do that is to grow, and show you all the good parts. We will learn together.

"How are you finding motherhood?"

"I love it! It's so fun and beautiful, I-"

"Shhhhh, don't say that."

Huh? I was shhh'd for enjoying motherhood? I can't tell if they're joking.

The same people who laughed when I was miserable pregnant and 'warned' me about how hard parenting is, don't want to hear how things have changed?

All I want to do is boast to the world about how much I love you and how much I love being your mother, so that's what I do. Perhaps that's what has inspired all of these pages.

Thank you for grabbing my finger today.

You fart with the power of an adult. I had to double check: was it you, or your dad?

How did you do that?

I laugh. Farts are funny.

I wake up in the middle of the night. You're OK. I just can't sleep. I realise I'm *finally* breathing through my nose. It isn't blocked.

I inhale just because, and appreciate the snot-free oxygen I am able to take in.

I go back to sleep and when we wake up, I feel well rested. That was the best sleep I've had in months.

'Pregnancy tired' is worse than 'newborn tired'.

No matter how much I would rest or sleep while pregnant, I always felt like I'd never slept in my life.

But newborn tired, you're here. You're not growing inside me draining my energy.

You're demanding of having your needs met, sure. But who isn't? The privilege of meeting those needs, of being the one to soothe and nourish you, feels like the biggest gift.

One night I walk in to see your dad holding you, soothing you to music with tears in his eyes.

"Are you OK?"

"She will never be this tiny again. She's so beautiful."

You are so loved.

The part where I worried about my marriage? Gone.

I have never been more in love with him than I am now.

I am determined to show you what love looks like, so you never question if it's there and never question if you're worthy.

You get the hiccups all the time, just like when you were in my belly.

Your little body jolts with each hic.

I felt these for months. Now we get to experience them on

the outside.

I had assumed you would be bothered by them. But, strangely enough, you fall asleep as if they're rocking you.

You wake from a nap, crying, rooting around looking for boob.

I feed you. At least I try.

My nipple is in your mouth but you're still running your head side to side, mouth wide open.

"It's in your mouth… close your mouth."

I giggle. I find it funny.

Imagine if adults ate like this.

You're 3 days old, and it's day two of having you home. One of our cats attacked the other. It has happened before but not this bad. We make the heart breaking decision to re-home him. We don't need the stress of catty chaos while learning how to be parents.

I cry.

And I cry again.

Actually, I didn't stop crying for about 2 days.

I love animals. I have never re-homed a pet. Instead, I have adopted 3. I feel so much guilt and shame in having to re-home him.

And I feel that guilt and shame all over again for letting it impede on my time with you.

For the first time in years, I cry to my mum.

"I can take him."

My mum is having renovations done but she can take him when the house is finished.

What will we do until then?

Your dad asks his mum if she can take him for a few months.

She also says yes.
I feel incredible relief, but the guilt still lingers.

You're struggling to latch properly. Breastfeeding is painful. My nipples are blistered, scabbed and bloody. You feed and my body tenses. You have lost 10% of your body weight. I need a break. I need to bottle feed but I don't want to. I feel like I have let you down. I cry.

With some help from a lactation consultant, we find out that you have a tongue tie.
I didn't know much about them until now.
You are latching as well as you can, but we decide to book you in for a tongue tie release in a week. Until then, I will pump breast milk and your dad and I will bottle feed you.

"Now *anyone* can feed her", someone says.
No thank you. Feeding my baby is *my* job. It's my joy. Just because I'm using a bottle now does not invite anyone to do so. Especially when I have no other choice at the moment.
I feel very protective over this.
Hormones? Instinct?
I don't know, but I want to breastfeed again, soon.

Despite the pain, I love breast feeding. What a privilege to be the one who provides you with nourishment and comfort. What an incredible system of nature this is. I feel lucky that I can.
Quiet bonding for just the two of us.
I hope that the next few days help.

Notes to my Daughter

I pump breast milk for a few days. These days are the hardest.

Keeping up with your demands, making sure there's enough milk for day, night and cluster feeds. Most of the time I'm ahead. Then cleaning up the bottles and pump parts to be ready for your next order. Far out.

The nights are tricky. Your dad and I both need to wake. Your dad takes the night shift for feeds and I pump, again.

During these nights we put "Mr Bean" on the TV.

We are delirious. It makes us laugh. We go back to sleep.

It's just what we need for those 2am feeds.

Three days of expressing breast milk and bottle feeding. You gained the weight back.

I try to breastfeed again. It's a little bit uncomfortable, but not unbearably painful.

I'm so glad that the 3 day break helped.

You're booked in to have your tongue tie released next week.

Somewhere in between all the pumping:

You haven't pooped since leaving the hospital and I haven't pooped since your birth.

Overnight I feel the urge. I get up and walk to the bathroom. When I stand I realise how strong gravity is and how weak my pelvic floor is.

I poo myself.

I cry and laugh to your dad.

He cleans me up… and the floor… Oops.

What a humbling experience.

At least no-one ever needs to know…

He doesn't make me feel bad, not once.

When you wake up, you also do your first poo since being

home.
 Dadda cleans that, too.
 I married a wonderful man.

Your dad already does so much for us. He does everything except breastfeed. Though I'm sure he would if he could. At this point he has changed more nappies than I have. Actually, he is the only one who has changed your nappies so far.
 He has given you your first bath.
 He dresses you.
 He burps you.
 He rocks you to sleep.
 He keeps the house tidy.
 He makes us food.
 He brings me water and makes me coffee.
 He makes sure you and I are safe and loved.
 We love him.

You sleep for 3-4 hours during the day. We need to wake you up for feeding.
 Otherwise, we sit with you and snuggle on the couch together. We watch Netflix. A lot.
 I think we finish it.

You are made of velcro. Your preference is to be held.
 You will tolerate just enough tummy time or being on your play mat.
 When you cry, I respond with love.
 I refuse to let you cry it out, or to let you ever feel alone or feel like you won't receive love from me.
 I hold you when you want to be held.

Notes to my Daughter

All of your naps are contact naps.
You're fed on demand.
If I can help it, you will never feel alone and you will always know safety.

A week later and you cry and scream when your tongue tie is released.
You latch better immediately, though momentarily.
It will take some time for you to get used to this. Me too.
We will learn together.

One day the 3 of us are at brunch. I love doing things as a family.
Your dad and I are talking about how lucky we are to have you and to have time off from work.
The conversation shifts to the future and potentially giving you a sibling.
Your dad is excited at the thought, talking about how wonderful it will be and how much he loves being your dad.
While he is talking I start to cry.
"Are you OK?"
"It was so hard."
That's all I can get out. It's hard to talk about. It's hard to re-live. It's hard to write about.
One day we might have another child. Until then, having you is a blessing and I'm incredibly grateful.

I don't think other people understand that this subject is upsetting.
Conversations are thrown around all the time about me being pregnant again and future kids. Bringing up a subject that I feel is traumatic, without concern for my health, dismissing what I

went through and how it makes me feel.

Often I stay quiet or walk away.

I don't want the pressure to re-live it.

Again, I choose to focus on what I have.

Traumatic. Is that the right word? It seems big and heavy.

But the more I re-live it, the more I think it's appropriate to use.

I remember feeling parts of me shatter and slip away with each passing hour of labour.

I remember the point in which all my preparation had unravelled and I could no longer breathe.

I remember the feeling of fighting my own body while walking down that hallway - my vision had gone blurry, my hearing went dull and I was trying not to collapse… or vomit.

I remember feeling like my body was failing or like I was failing my body. I'm not sure which.

I remember feeling utterly exhausted from labour and pushing for 2 hours. Only to continue pushing for another hour before forceps were shoved inside me to rip my baby out.

I remember feeling terrified knowing that I was going to be cut, despite being fully informed prior.

I remember feeling the pressure of my baby coming out and of the doctor's weight pulling her out.

I remember the fear in those moments, looking helplessly to my husband for help, but fully knowing he couldn't do anything.

And painfully, when the anaesthetist told me the epidural may (unlikely) fail, I remember thinking *"I'd rather die"*, and truly preferring that option.

The thought of doing all of that again, or not getting an epidural in time makes me shake. I can feel my heart race as if it is happening again.

So yes. Perhaps 'Traumatic' *is* the correct word.

Now, when people ask "When is baby number two coming?"

I just say "I'm still recovering from baby one. Thanks for asking."

I have always been a very light sleeper, and I'm very in tune to you.

"Is she sleeping in the bassinet?"

"No, she sleeps with us."

Some people look horrified.

"Aren't you worried you'll roll on her?"

"If I was worried, I wouldn't do it."

Times have changed and so has advice.

We set ourselves up safely. We still follow safe sleep guidelines.

You don't need to cry to get my attention at night.

When you're hungry all you need to do is reach for me and I'm there. Your rooting reflex kicks in, you get milk immediately, and you go back to sleep.

There is no in and out of bed, in between cold and warm, or re-settling back to sleep.

You're safe and you know it.

When you need me all you need to do is reach for me. I will never regret that.

"Isn't co-sleeping dangerous?"

Isn't it dangerous to be sleep deprived?

"Aren't you worried she will be sleeping with you until she's a

toddler?"
So what if she does?

"It will create bad habits."
Like feeling safe?

"She's manipulating you."
Her brain hasn't developed nearly enough to understand what manipulation is, but OK.

"You're going to spoil her."
By meeting her basic human needs? Impossible.

Deliberate, planned out co-sleeping is not dangerous - but falling asleep, unprepared while exhausted, is. Humans are the only mammals that are told *not* to sleep with their babies.
Safe co-sleeping is the best advice we have received.

I chose to bring life into this world. I am not going to leave you in a dark, empty room and leave you to cry.
As adults, if we come across someone who is upset or in need, we don't ignore them. Or at least we shouldn't. So why would I shut out my own baby?

Only a few people are curious and support our sleeping arrangements. They ask how it's going and I can't boast fast enough:
"Amazing! She sleeps 8pm – 8am. She feeds but goes straight back to sleep. No fuss. I haven't slept this well in months!"
I'm glad people ask.

Notes to my Daughter

When we rest in side lying you do this thing:
You finish feeding, pull away and tilt your head up to the ceiling. That's my cue. Then I squish in more and you rest your head back down. You use my boob as a pillow. It's super cute.

You use me as a dummy, though won't actually take a dummy. I'm not complaining.
I provide you with comfort and you provide fulfilment.
My heart is so full.

You're about 4 weeks old when it's our one year wedding anniversary.
It's surreal that your dad and I used to talk about a life with you, and now you're here.
It's so much better than we ever thought it could be.

You're 5 weeks old for my first Mothers Day. You and your dad spoil me.
I am so grateful to be celebrating this day.
The best gift is you.

When I was pregnant people would say "Just wait until the baby is here."
As if to say 'you haven't experienced hard yet'.
As if to discount my experience or put fear into my experience of motherhood.

And as much as I cannot put into words how much I hated pregnancy, I equally cannot put into words how much I love being a mother.

Notes To You

From the moment I gave birth I felt the best I'd felt in 40 weeks.

All my pregnancy symptoms went away and I felt more like myself with immediate relief and love.

The first night with you I literally did not sleep a wink.

I did not feel exhausted and I did not mind at all.

I was and still am obsessed with you and getting up to feed you feels like the biggest privilege. What an honour it is for you to believe that being in my arms is the safest place in the world.

Thank you for choosing me to be your mum.

When you're 6 weeks old, it's my birthday. (This is a busy month for your dad!)

You and Dadda sing me a little birthday song and he is on nappy duty today.

Your dad books for us to go to dinner and a massage. I can't wait.

You stay home with your grandma.

By the time we get to the massage I have been away from you for a few hours.

My boobs are engorged.

I lay face down on the massage table. Ouch. I hadn't considered the pressure on my boobs. It hurts!

The massage lady comes in and she climbs on my back. I had not thought this far ahead when I thought about a massage. I hadn't thought to tell them that I'm post partum. I feel like my boobs are going to explode.

Note to self: I can't lay on my stomach yet.

When we get home, you feed and it feels like someone popped a cork on a champagne bottle.

Sweet relief.

Notes to my Daughter

When you're feeding you pull away during let down.
 You get sprayed in the face.
 You look at me with a judgemental side-eye as if I do it on purpose.
 Such judgement.
 Sometimes it's milk, sometimes it's moisturiser.
 I see your little face covered in white milky drops - it's silly and cute.
 It makes me smile.

There was one occasion where we went to visit your grandma. Your dad picked your outfit and dressed you up. We arrived and your grandma took you for a cuddle.
 "Her bum feels thin… is she wearing a nappy?"
 Surely you are.
 No.
 Luckily you hadn't done a poo or wee during the drive over.
 Your dad puts a nappy on you and moments later you do a squelchy fart.
 We all laugh. What good timing!

You are starting to recognise us and smile when you see us.
 Your gummy smile is bright and beautiful.
 My heart melts.

Every week your latch gets better.
 I no longer feel the pain.
 I'm so proud of you.
 We make a good team.

You smile and giggle in your sleep. Sometimes you whimper.

Is it a bad dream?
You're only a few weeks old.
What do you dream of?
What makes you happy?
What makes you sad?
What scares you?
I wish you could tell me.

I love it when you get excited and kick your legs and flail your arms.
The little wobbles that come with it are adorable.

You have had a few days of inconsolable crying.
You get so upset that you won't feed.
My boobs hurt from being engorged, which makes it harder for you to feed, which hurts more… The cycle goes on.
I'm sorry I don't know how to help.
I'm learning too.
As loud and as sad as you are, I don't mind. I'm on leave to take care of you. I have nothing else I'd rather be doing.

I hear you cry - I set myself up ready to feed you and tell you, "Your cry is very important to me. You are the next baby in the queue."
Lucky there's no other babies lining up!

You've been crying for over an hour, nothing seems to help.
I decided to give you a bath. Why not?
It works. You stop crying and smile.
Bliss.
You stay in the water until it starts to go cold. I see your little

chin shiver.
I take you out and wrap you up.
You cry again.

We discover you love white noise.
Specifically, you find comfort in the vacuum cleaner.
You cry, we vacuum, you stop crying.
We stop vacuuming, you start crying… The floors have never been so clean!
We aren't sure if it's a coincidence.
It isn't.
We test and re-test over a few crying cycles.
Every time the vacuum is on, you settle.
It's funny and makes us laugh.

Each time you wake up from a sleep or a nap, we greet you with "Happy waking!"
You seem to love it. You smile every time you wake and hear it.

It's crazy how strong you are.
We still need to support your neck, but the strength is in your arms and legs.
Trying to get you dressed is a work out.
Straighten your leg!
Let go of your sleeve!
Bend your elbow!
Oh my gosh.
At this point, I'm starting to doubt if I would win in an arm wrestle despite your tiny size!

Your Dad and I have a race to see who can change your nappy the fastest.

Whoever gets the fastest time doesn't change your nappy for 48 hours.

Ready, set, go:

I clock 1 minute and 6 seconds. It was a *very* pooey nappy.

We wait for another pooey nappy.

Your dad gets 42 seconds. In my opinion it was a *mildly* pooey nappy.

I lose, and your dad has 2 days of nappy freedom.

Rigged.

Today you defy gravity.

You're contact napping on your dad, chest to chest.

You fart.

It's a poo.

It goes up your back.

Up? How?

It's everywhere.

It takes about 12 weeks for you to get the pattern of bedtime.

You're a brilliant sleeper, but you're also a victim of witching hour.

What is it about the early night that you find unsettling?

For at least an hour or two each night, we put on music and dance to try ease the crying.

Do you like it? Yes.

Do you stop crying? Yes.

You enjoy the evening discos until you're ready to shut your eyes.

The party's over for another night.

Notes to my Daughter

When you are content you tuck your chin to your chest and just chill out.

Your cheeks are squishy and we can see your double chin.
Dad and I call this 'Blob Fish Mode'.
If it's oddly quiet I will ask, "Is she asleep?"
"Nah she's just being a blob."

You slowly learn to laugh – my favourite sound in the world.

You haven't belly laughed yet, just a few little chuckles.
Sometimes you start to laugh but you stop and cry.
Did you scare yourself with that new noise?

You have your first illness.

Your nose is so blocked you can't feed properly.

You are so tired, but you don't have a fever. You sleep all day and night for a while.

If only you could blow your nose.

We use the snot sucker to try help with the congestion, but it doesn't do too much.

My poor baby.

With your extra sleeping, comes extra cuddles. I'll hold you until you feel better.

On Wednesday's I take us to *Mum & Bub* pilates. The first few classes you are not impressed. I put you on a blanket next to me to play. You don't appreciate not being held. I hold you for the whole class. A few times.

I don't mind. We can still do the exercises.

One day, you are very content with playing and watching me.

Of course it was on the day with a hard class. I could have used the break.

But instead I look at you and you coo at me. Like you're cheering me on.

Thank you, cheeky girl.

I like horror movies.

Sometimes you stare and smile at the air vent on the ceiling. It's very cute.

Until I think too much about it. What can you see in there?

Probably nothing.

I have realised we swaddled you for the last time. I don't know when it was, but it occurs to me that I haven't seen your little wraps for a while.

I want to go get a wrap and swaddle you now. But you're probably too long for them.

You loved being swaddled. My heart feels sad for the end of that phase. And momentarily sad for all of the things I will unknowingly do with you for the last time and not know it.

They're right, time does go fast. But it just makes me want to be present and savour these moments even more.

I'm going through your cupboard organising your clothes. You're fitting in to 00 now, so I get these out. In among the 00 clothes, I find a 0000.

Oh no.

An adorable onesie you'll never wear. You're far too big for it now.

I must have mistakenly put it in the wrong pile.

I feel another silly little heart break. What a shame.

I look through all of your clothing piles to make sure I haven't made the mistake again.

Notes to my Daughter

I think of my midwives often.
 Looking after me while pregnant and preparing me for birth.
 For spending over 12 hours with me in hospital during labour and birth.
 For making me feel safe and supported during my most vulnerable time.
 To them I'm one of many, part of their job.
 To me, they were phenomenal and I'll never forget them.
 'Thank you' isn't enough.

You're starting to reach for my face while you feed. I thought it would be annoying, but it isn't. It's sweet. You reach for me, I tell you "thank you" and kiss your hand.
 Your fingers land half in my mouth. You keep them there. I don't mind.

You are smiling more and more. I love your gummy smile. You don't have teeth yet and your breath is milky. Something about this combination is just heaven.

I have never been more happy to make a fool of myself if the reward is your smile.
 I dance around the kitchen to music. You love it.
 I think.

You love movement.
 Walking while being held.
 Moving in the pram.
 Moving in the car.
 If the car stops, you tell me all about it. When we move again, you stop crying.

When we stop I explain to you that sometimes we have to. Like for red lights or pedestrians. But you obviously don't understand.

Every stop let's out a cry within seconds. And every start up, your cries ease.

Kind of like with the vacuum.

You start to find your voice. You coo and screech and yell and scream.

It's wonderful. Every milestone you hit I think, 'You're a genius'.

You'll be ready to give a motivational speech by tomorrow.

We talk to each other often, sharing stories about the day.

I hope you grow up knowing you can tell me anything.

Your dad and I go to see a movie and your grandma baby sits you again.

We are so lucky to have so much family close by.

It's a superhero movie with a superhero baby.

The superhero baby cries.

My boobs think they can help.

They leak.

I realise I forgot to wear pads in my bra.

When the movie ends I see that half my top is still wet.

Oh well.

"What's something you're looking forward to doing with your babies when they're older?"

A question asked to our First Time Parent Group.

"I'm looking forward to taking her to feed the ducks… and walking over crunchy leaves together!"

Notes to my Daughter

I can't choose just one.
Both feel incredibly wholesome to think about.

Someone asks me about going back to work.
It's still a long while away.
But, ugh.
I never thought I would want to spend so much time on leave with you.
"You don't like your job?"
I do. It's not that.
It's that I will never find any other job, or any other use of my time that will feel more fulfilling or make my heart this happy.
Maybe I could write a book.
Hmm…

Now that you are recognising more, when I feed you, you stop feeding to look at me.
It's like you're checking if I'm still here.
You smile and feed again.
Then you stop and look…
It's a cycle.
"I promise you, I cannot leave while you're drinking."
You don't understand.
But you smile.
You drink.
You pull away and look.
"I'm still here, baby."
We smile at each other.
This continues for a while.
Because you're pulling away, milk is dripping down my body and spraying on your face.

This game is messy but fun.

I'm not sure who's winning, but you make me feel like I am.

You have started to realise we bring you comfort.

When I hold you and rock you to sleep you pull back and look at me. You see my face, recognise me, smile, then bury your face in my chest again.

You do this to your dad too. It's heartwarming.

On the exhale of your yawns you do a little "oh".

Dramatic, sweet, innocent, cute.

I love it.

You're asleep on your dad.

I hear him whisper to you, "You are beautiful. You are clever."

"Is she awake?"

"No. I want her to hear it in her dreams."

My heart melts.

"I can feel her bottom teeth!" Your dad tells me.

Oh my goodness, you have little white nubs on your bottom gums.

No wonder you have been extra chewy and slobbery lately.

The next night you seem unsettled and in pain.

We go to give you some baby Panadol but the bottle was sideways and the lid was not on properly.

It's leaked out.

There's a little bit in the bottle that we manage to give you, but you spit half out.

We soothe you as much as we can before bed.

We go to change your nappy, but there's none left.

Notes to my Daughter

How did we over look this?

Oh no.

What a series of events.

There are some smaller size nappies in the car. They're better than nothing.

We use one of those overnight. In the morning we get more nappies and Panadol.

One day while teething you have a fit of pain. Out of nowhere you cry and cry.

Our hearts break. All we want to do is take the pain away.

Panadol hasn't helped and the vacuum is out of battery.

I'm sorry we can't fix it.

We would if we could.

Your dad decides to carry you while pretending to vacuum. He moves the vacuum back and forth while humming.

The crying stops.

I laugh, but really I'm just glad it soothes you.

Breastfeeding while you're teething is a roll of the dice.

Will I get a new piercing today? Will I loose my nipple?

I hope not.

Sometimes you chomp down and pull... Not only that, but you turn your head side to side like a shark.

Argh.

I tell you 'no' and take the boob away. You chew on your toys instead.

You learn quickly and bite me only a few times.

One day we are listening to music in the living room. I'm dancing, you love it. You wobble and smile as you watch. You start to kick your leg. Just one. It's like you're doing a knee wack to the music. Even funnier, it's in time to the beat. It makes me laugh a lot.

You do the knee wack most times music comes on.

It's your signature dance move.

We go to dinner at your grandma's house. We drive there over the time of your last nap of the day. Your nap is disturbed and you sleep for maybe 5 minutes. You're very tired.

I try to rock you to sleep before dinner. I haven't looked at you in a while but you haven't fidgeted much.

I think you're asleep.

I look down.

Your eyes are as wide as an owls just staring at me.

Oh no.

Then you smile and coo and fidget.

I look away and continue to try help you sleep.

You stop moving and stop making noise.

About 10 more minutes go by before I check to see if you're asleep yet.

Do I dare look?

I do.

Your eyes wide again, already locked on to me.

You smile instantly again and kick your legs.

You don't go to sleep until we get home.

Little con artist.

I love your little wobbles.

Everything is so new to you, even being upright and stabilising yourself.

Notes to my Daughter

We are with some friends, and I am holding you upright. We are all talking and then your dad lets out a belly laugh. You jolt and wobble, your bottom lip pouts and you cry. We keep laughing at your little startle. I keep holding you close and you calm down.

I love how everything you see, hear and do, is for the first time. Not just rolling over, crawling, walking, eating, speaking…

But the little things too.

Like the first time you went outside, your first car ride, the first time you heard a sneeze and got scared, the first time you felt wind on your face.

Your little reactions are the best thing to witness.

One day you will feel grass on your feet and sand between your toes. You'll get splashed by a wave and probably get spooked.

Being present for these things is one of my favourite things about parenting. These little moments feel bigger than the milestones.

We took you to the Aquarium today.

You loved the blue lights and watching the fish swim around.

Your head moved from side to side as you tracked the fish. I was surprised at how well you were tracking.

You are *so* full of wonder and curiosity.

Your dad holds you close to the glass and your hands rest against it.

You don't know what this invisible barrier is.

You lean your head forward to see more.

But you bonk your face on the glass.

You cry.

We give you cuddles straight away.
You're fine, no injury.
You're happy spending the rest of the time in your dad's arms.
I love seeing you learn about the world.

You're 5 months old when your dad goes back to work.

He has had a lot of time off with us and it's been *incredible*. I am extremely grateful that we both have jobs which allow us to have this time to raise you.

People ask how I'm feeling about your dad going back to work. Honestly I feel fine about it. The 3 of us have had a wonderful 5 months. We have followed your lead to build a good routine and I feel confident in knowing your cues. If your dad went back to work after a week or 2, I would be extremely anxious.

On your dad's first day at work, he gets out of bed at 6am and you sleep in until 7:30am. Ah, bliss already. You and I go for a walk around the lake, and find a gift for your dad for Fathers Day, which is on the coming weekend. It's a lovely day and you stay in your sleep routine. We hang out and I love it.

When your dad comes home you smile when you see his face and do happy kicks with your legs. I love that you are starting to recognise people!

We are both happy to have Dadda home for the rest of the day.

I put you in your first dress for Fathers Day. "Wow baby! Look at you!" Your dad tells you as he gives you a big hug. We give him his gifts and have a lovely day with our family.

Your dad is the perfect dad for you. He loves you so much.

Notes to my Daughter

From the moment you were born he has been wrapped around your little finger. He will always support you and protect you. I hope your dad knows how much we appreciate him. You and I will make him feel loved every day.

"Happy Fathers Day, Dadda!

Mumma says love at first sight is real because of the way you looked at me when I was born. You loved me straight away and I love you right back. I held your finger, you held me so close and told me "You're Dadda's girl." And I am.

Sometimes I dream that I can hear you tell me you love me. Do you whisper to me while I'm sleeping?

I love it when we get to play, you put a big smile on my face and make me laugh! But just a little bit because sometimes I spook myself when I laugh too big. I'm still learning.

Thank you for teaching me everything I know so far. I'm watching and learning from you every day.

I hear other people call you a funny name, but I'll just call you Dadda.

Love, Dadda's Girl."

Today I was showing you yourself in the mirror. You would smile at me, then see our reflection and smile again. Do you think you have 2 mums? Real mum and mirror mum? I wonder what you think when you see another 'mum' in front of you. You keep it up, looking and smiling between the two.

I held you to the mirror again today but you didn't look away from me. Real me. Instead of looking at our reflection you stared at me for what felt like forever. Your little face went from smiling, to shocked, to relaxed... and cycled all over again. Then you put your hands on my face and felt around. It was like you were really seeing me for the first time. Like something out of a movie or a first encounter. I kept waiting for your focus to break and the moment to be over. Surely this is an accident? Maybe it was. But you just kept looking at me, smiling and gently touching.

Something then felt immeasurably special.

That moment will forever be one of my favourites.

We had our first game of chase this evening. Your dad was holding you and you smiled at me when I walked past. "I'm gonna get ya!" I said as I dance my fingers forward at you. You made a coo as if you understood, so I hopped forward and tickled you. You smile and half laugh. I walk away, spot you from across the room and say "I'm gonna get ya!" The cycle repeats, but this time your dad carries you away. "No, you can't get me!" We chase each other through the house while you smile and coo. When you are being chased you screech as if you understand.

We play this game for a while, and again over the next few days and beyond. Each time you have the same reaction. I love watching you learn.

Tonight I'm making dinner. Nothing fancy, just satay chicken and rice.

The chicken is diced and the pan is hot. I scrape the chicken into the pan.

No I don't.

I scrape the chicken into the *bin*.

No!

Notes to my Daughter

What have I done?
Is pregnancy brain lingering? Is it mum brain?
This is so dumb.
I lose about half the chicken.
Ugh.

When I was pregnant, part of my self doubt was around daily activity. I love being active and made time for that each day. Apart from that your dad and I are very much home bodies. We love video games, board games, movies. I would think:
'Where will I find the energy to do things with you?'
'Will I want to take you places?'
Yes.
It turns out I love taking you out and doing things with you. I involve you in as much as I can, even if it's mundane house work. You hang out with me and I just narrate what I'm doing. You usually coo back and we have a chat.
We go for walks, we go to see family, we go to brunch.
In no way do you feel like a burden. I never want you to feel like you are.

One day we take you to an exhibit at the museum.
Do you have any idea what it's about? No.
Will you remember? No.
Did you have fun? I don't know, but I did.

One afternoon we walk to Bunnings and we buy some flowers and fairy themed garden ornaments.
When we get home we go to the backyard and you watch me as I plant the flowers in some coloured pots. I put out the ornaments near by and call it your 'Fairy Corner'.

You don't know what it is.

You won't interact with it for a year or two.

But I just love involving you in life.

As I'm arranging the pots, some birds fly over head and chirp. They catch your attention, and you look up in wonder searching for the noise.

"What was that, baby?"

I don't think you can see the birds. The trees they flew into are very tall and full. But you keep looking anyway with awe on your face.

I show you the Fairy Corner when I'm finished. I think you liked the birds more.

But you're happy all the same.

I see a video online: *"Kissing your baby increases their oxytocin which helps with safe bonding and attachment. It reduces cortisol which reduces their stress."* ... *"Babies who receive more love and affection in their early years grow a bigger hippocampus. That's the part of the brain responsible for memory and emotion."*

I kiss you 28,000 times.

"You're going to have the biggest hippocampus!"

It's our new compliment we tell you now.

I have a funny vision of you going to your first day of school and telling the teachers and kids: "My mum says I have a big hippocampus!"

Last week I tore my lower oblique muscle. I was walking and tripped. I didn't fall but I awkwardly tried to re-balance, and here we are.

It hurt a lot and it certainly was not on my bingo card for post-partum recovery. I'm already seeing a physio for my pelvic floor, I may as well throw in a torn abdominal muscle.

It isn't the worst thing in the world, but I'm sad I need to take a few days break from picking you up and going for walks.

Your dad is making dinner - steak and veggies. "Should I mash some sweet potato for her?"

You're almost 6 months old. "Sure, let's try!"

We have a 'dummy' with holes, which you can disassemble and put food in. Your dad puts some mashed sweet potato inside and gives it to you. You taste it and make a face as if you're eating a sour lemon, and you wobble.

Funny girl.

"What's that flavour?"

We let you know you're doing a good job.

You go back for more, and make more faces. Then go back for more, and more faces…

You don't love it, but you don't hate it.

First food done.

The next day we try some blueberries.

You like these better, until you get a sour one and make the lemon face again.

But you are much happier to chomp on the 'food dummy' with blueberries than you were with the sweet potato.

Blueberries are a hit.

Today was another of my favourite moments.

I was holding you and you were cooing. We were talking to each other.

"You've got the biggest hippocampus I've ever seen!"

You put your hands on my neck and bury your face into me,

then stay there for a moment.
  Is this your version of a hug?
  Maybe.
  Maybe not.
  But I love it.

I forgot I like boiled eggs.
  Hey, I have something to help me make them.
  I get out the egg boiling machine.
  I put 2 eggs in and they come out perfectly.
  Yum.
  Finally I made boiled eggs on my own. It only took 31 years.
  I guess I'm finally on my way to knowing everything.

You have been trying to feed with your hand in your mouth. Your fingers break the suction and latch. It doesn't work. But you get upset if I move your hand.
  Another messy game. I guess I need to start getting used to these games we play… and the messes.

One afternoon your dad takes you for a nappy change. I can hear the 2 of you giggling and blowing raspberries together. Then I hear "AH! You pooed on me!"
  I run upstairs.
  Your dad was giving you raspberries on your belly while your nappy was off. You laughed and projectile pooed on him.
  I can't stop laughing and I'm barely able to help clean up.
  Sorry, Dadda.

You're starting to sit on your own! Big strong baby.
  Every now and then you reach your arm out and twirl your

wrist around. Have you just realised you have hands? You look at them in wonder. Your fingers do an uncoordinated dance grabbing at nothing. What are you doing? Funny little thing.

You find your feet shortly after you find your hands. You try and lean forward to taste them but they don't lift up to your mouth. You get irritated and cry. After a few weeks you become quite flexible and get a taste.

I'm impressed.

I feel you wake up in the mornings. Sometimes I lay next to you with my eyes closed to try to encourage you to go back to sleep. It works about half the time.

When it *doesn't* work, you coo and babble, but softly. It's as if you know you should be whispering.

Did I teach you that?

If, by this point I haven't 'woken up' yet, you have started to put your hand on my face and tap your fingers on my cheek. I melt. It's *so* sweet. I *have* to 'wake up' when you do it.

I open my eyes and see you. You see my eyes open, smile at me and do an excited screech.

Then we start our day.

You give every surface you touch a little grab and scratch, including my face. One day all of these little things will just stop.

For now, they're beautiful ways that you explore the world.

I sit you in my lap and we read a book together. You look at each page and reach out for them. You grab a page as I turn it and you help - you turned your first page, and you know it.

Notes To You

You do a screech and excited little huffs.

   I love that you love reading.

There is one evening where your dad and I go to dinner. Your grandma looks after you and when we pick you up, you have Elmo socks on. Only the Elmo on your socks is green, not red. Your dad says "Cute Gromice socks, miss!"

Gromice?

"Do you mean Gromit? Or Grimace?"

"I dunno, whoever the green guy is in the trash can."

"Oscar the Grouch?"

"Oh. Yeah."

"Who is Gromice?"

   We still have no idea. But we call these socks your Gromice socks anyway.

One weekend we have the family over for a board game day. This will be a regular occurrence as you grow up. I wonder what games you will like… Will you like strategy? Will you like chaos? Will you like building? Will you like trading? I Can't wait to find out!

   When your grandma arrives, she brings you a bubble machine. We take you outside and turn it on. Your aunty, uncle, cousins and grandmas come too and watch with anticipation. Then bubbles fly everywhere, way too many to count. Your eyes grow wide and your head moves around trying to track them all. I know I've said it before, but these moments are magical. Your little arms reach out trying to grab them. We all can't help but smile while witnessing the magic.

You are doing really well with trying new foods. You love steak and a close second is tomato. Who would have thought? I give you wedges of tomato and a few minutes later only the skin is left.

We have noticed that you reach for food and your toys mostly with your left hand. The knee wack you do, is also with your left leg. Is it too early to tell if you'll be left handed?

There's one night where we have dinner a bit later than usual. You're sucking the juice out of a strip of steak, then your head dips and you start to nod off.

"Let's go to bed, Bubba."

We go to bed and all of a sudden it's raspberry o'clock.

Thhbbbbbbbb...

What happened to my baby who was so tired she couldn't eat?

Thhbbbbbbbb! Thbb thbb thbb!

OK. Well I guess this is what we are doing now, until you get tired again.

When you're about 6 months old, the 3 of us travel interstate for another wedding. This is a bit of a wild ride so bare with me:

We had a plane trip and had to arrive at 6:15am.

The night before leaving, you were very unwell. You were sick and fussy, you went to bed late and woke up in the night frequently.

We packed our bags the morning of leaving. I don't know why we felt like that was a good idea after the night we all had.

Your grandma picked us all up and took us to the airport.

Your dad says, "I'll take her and get our tickets. You go ahead with the backpack and pram."

I went through the gate with our things and I got a thousand questions. "Is all of this yours?", "Where is the baby?"

"With my husband getting tickets…"

What was going on?

They put our bags through the scanner twice and went over the pram with a metal detector. They questioned me several times about why I had bags, a pram but no baby. I promised them you were around the corner with your dad, coming at any moment.

Finally they let me through but not without some suspicious looks.

Then I check my phone and see a text:

"Come back. We missed the flight."

Fuck.

We didn't have to be here at 6:15am… Our plane *took off* at 6:15am…

After being in the firing line of questioning and promising that my husband and baby were coming, all the workers watched me awkwardly walk back through the gates.

I find you and your dad, "The tickets were non-refundable."

Double fuck.

My heart sinks.

Your dad looks online and finds the next available flight. "It's at 9:45am."

"Great, lets check in right now."

The lady at the check in desk says, "I'm sorry but I can't see that flight."

She does some digging, and, "That flight is for 3 days from now."

Triple fuck?

I cry. We can't afford to buy tickets *again*.

These flights *were* refundable though. So your dad spent some time on the phone trying to re-book the flights.

Our flight was finally booked for the *correct* day at 12:30pm. We had about 5 hours to spare.

Your grandma and granddad worked close by so we went to see them, and get coffee, and saw your grandparents again… and got another coffee…

We checked in to the gate 1 hour and 30 minutes early and finally got on our flight.

You were brilliant with the flying. You were dozy while we were taking off and had fallen asleep before the seat belt sign was turned off. You stayed asleep for the whole flight.

Anyway, in the end it was a gorgeous trip and a beautiful wedding.

I don't think we will be travelling again for a while though.

You have exited the phase of putting your fingers in your mouth while you breastfeed, but now you're in a new phase - with your top arm you grab and squeeze my other boob as you eat. You make a fist with my boob in your hand… I didn't know my boobs could be crumpled like paper until now.

When fighting sleep after a feed, you also sometimes flick and scrunch my nipples.

Thanks.

It feels pretty gross but I am impressed with your fine motor skills.

I have started to pat you to sleep. I put my hand your chest and tap my finger lightly like a heart beat.

Tap-tap… Tap-tap…

You seem to like it.

You grab my hand and I feel your grip slowly loosen as you

fall asleep.
Tap-tap... Tap-tap...

Changing your nappy has become an Olympic sport, though I don't know if I mean for you or me. Probably both.

Toes in mouth, grabbing your nappy, your hands in your business, twisting and rolling around, grabbing yourself before I can wipe.

Poo poo fingers... Yuck.

I'd like to see your dad change your nappy in 42 seconds now.

Your next teeth to come in are your canines. You have a gap in the front and little vampire teeth instead. It's a few weeks before Halloween when they start to come in, very aptly timed, my little vampire.

Not long after, come your front teeth. Oh my God you have 6 teeth by 6 and a half months old. How have you got more teeth than hairs on your head?

You have a day of pain and cluster-feeding. I don't bother putting a shirt on. Between feeds you grab and fiddle with my bra. You grip the fabric, pull my bra to the side and reveal my boob. Your eyes grow wide and you screech with excitement.

You just found gold... liquid gold!

If I'm ever stuck in a time loop, I hope it's in any of the stories within these pages.

At this point in time you are 7 and a half months old. I have several months of leave left with you. It's nearly your first Christmas. Your dad and I have never bothered with a

Notes to my Daughter

Christmas tree, until now. We get a brand new one with built in lights, along with some decorations. All 3 of us set it up in our living room and admire it together.

Every day I look forward to what lies ahead.

In case it hasn't been obvious, there is so much I love. I could keep writing, and maybe I will. But for now, this is where we are.

It only feels like last week I found out I was pregnant and just yesterday you were born. Tomorrow you will be walking. Next week you'll go to school and come home to tell me that you got your driver's license. You'll drive away on adventures, and I'll sit by the phone wondering when you'll have time to call. Then you'll come to visit and tell me you're engaged. Your wedding day will be here before we know it and you'll have your own children we will coo over together.

All in the blink of an eye.

People are right: time does go fast.

I want to remember everything and I want to be present.

I want to remember more than I can capture in photos and videos.

Like the screech of you finding your voice, your soft yawns, your little fingers wrapped around my thumb, your soft skin, your baby breath…

Maybe that's why I'm writing it down here.

So those moments that get lost in photos can remain timeless.

Now

There have been some difficulties. Nothing unmanageable. Everything is brand new. But even when you scream and cry, even when my nipples were scabbed, I have never wished you out of any phase.

Your dad is right. You will never be this small again.

One day when you're grown up, I will be a parent to an adult.

And I will be a parent to an adult for far longer than I was ever a parent to a child.

And I will have been a parent to a baby for an even shorter time.

I cherish every single beautiful and hard moment with you.

I think about how much anxiety consumed me while I was pregnant.

How much I was worried that I wouldn't love you when I met you.

How I doubted every single aspect of myself.

My only regret is the doubt.

Now

I cry.
Not out of doubt or anxiety - it doesn't win this time.
I cry for how happy I am.
I am so grateful for my life and my family.
I feel overwhelmed with love.

I don't claim to be cured of my anxiety. Not at all.
I know it's still there.
It's just that these days it's manageable and my priorities have shifted.
I know now that being a mother means that my heart lives outside of my body,
on her own two legs,
walking her own path.
And I can only hope that the world keeps her safe.

A Note to Myself

To the pre-mother version of myself:

Remember to love yourself and give yourself more grace. I know that is cliche and who knows what that really means? It's OK to rest, even if that is *all* you're doing. Truly. Not only are you growing a person but you're also growing an entirely new organ. Your body is prioritising this life, your blood volume has increased up to 50%, your organs are rearranging, your whole body and being is being disassembled… It's OK to hate that. Hate it as much as you want and need to. It does not change how much you will love your baby.

    I know you focus a lot on it, but there's more to you as a person and your worth than what size clothing you fit into or what the scale says.

    There are far more important things, and I promise you will see that soon.

    Soon you'll be soothing your tiny baby to sleep.

    She will be crying but she will stop when you hold her.

A Note to Myself

You will both be wearing nappies.
Your boobs will be leaking, and your tummy will be rolling.
You won't care.
Neither will she.
Your baby will snuggle into you, and you realise that *this* is all that matters.
This is everything you have ever wanted.

People will ask how you are, and you will say "Living the dream!"
You'll say it with pride and love, not sarcastically like people do.

Everything you wanted but thought you didn't deserve.
Everything that you convinced yourself you didn't want, because it was easier than being disappointed.
Everything that seemed so far away.
You get it.
And you live it every day.
Each morning you will wake up wanting to pinch yourself, but you don't need to.
And every day you wake up with gratitude that you get to call this life yours.
This is your version of rich.

A Note of Thanks

Neither of you might believe this, but despite the fact that I have written an entire memoir, I struggle to find the words.

My Husband,

I couldn't have done any of this without you.

Not just the making the baby part (ha), but any of it.

I couldn't have gotten through the pregnancy, miserable, without you to lean on, sometimes literally. You took my emotional and physical weight and made it ours. You never made me feel crazy, unloved or invalidated.

You always held space, you still do.

Thank you for your unwavering compassion, support and love. You make me feel seen beyond measure.

Mum,

Wow - is this how you felt when I was born?

Whenever I would say "I love you" and you replied "I love you more!", now I know you truly did, and do. Despite the

A Note of Thanks

immeasurable love I have for you, now I know the feeling of loving your baby.

Aside from wanting to share my truths of parenting, this has been inspired by you.

The never wavering love you have shown me all my life is what I aspire to give to your grandchild.

Everything I am and everything I hope to be, I owe to you.

Thank you both infinitely for showing me what love is.

Love, Beth x

Connection

I'm just a mother figuring out life with my husband and child.

In no way do I wish for this to discount anyone else's experience.

I hate some things that others loved, and I love some things that others hated.

I wish for this to offer love and hope to those who need it.

This is the perspective I wish I had when I was pregnant.

If motherhood has taught me anything, it is the power of connection.

I had hoped in writing this to heal parts of myself.

If along the way this resonates with someone else, or helps someone to feel less alone, that is a bonus.

I encourage anyone reading to reach out to appropriate support services if you need it.

For updates, reflections and more heartfelt bites, you can connect with me on Instagram: @BethsLittleNotes

www.ingramcontent.com/pod-product-compliance
Lightning Source LLC
Chambersburg PA
CBHW071250070526
44583CB00017B/2406